CONTENTS

		Pages
Compiler's introduction		4-6
Historical introduction		7-8
Brief chronology of North Lancashire & Cumbria tramways		9-12
Classification scheme		13
A	General works	14
B	Specific tramway systems	15-28
C	Works on other tramways	28
D	Light Rail Schemes	28
E	Tramway museums and preservation	28-30
F	Tramway manufacturers	31
G	Reference material	32-37
H	Library addresses	37-38
Publishing programme		38-39

COMPILER'S INTRODUCTION

In 1995 Adam Gordon and I got together to discuss various proposals for a bibliography of British tramways. Our original plan was for a single volume covering the whole country, but we eventually decided to try a regional approach. This is the seventh volume in the series, the earlier ones having dealt with the tramways of Scotland (1998), Wales (2000), North-East England (2001), Yorkshire (2002) East Anglia (2003) and South-Central England (2003).

The text of this publication is based on parts of a bibliography entitled "Tramways of Great Britain and Ireland" which I submitted for Fellowship of the Library Association in 1984, and which was subsequently accepted.

The original text consisted of books and periodical articles published between 1861 and 1981. Material published after 1981 was collated in a supplementary volume, and this has now been added to the original text, bringing coverage up to the end of 2002. No part of the work has been published previously.

To my original text Adam has contributed some further titles, and also material on tramway legislation, arbitration and accident reports. We hope that this guide will assist tramway enthusiasts and historians to make a more complete study of tramways, and that, in turn, more information will come to light on the interesting systems which existed.

How to use this guide
In order to set the scene, we have included an historical introduction to the relevant tramways, followed by a chronology listing the major tramway events.

The bibliography commences with general works, followed by works on specific tramway systems, arranged alphabetically by name. Within each section, the entries are arranged in chronological order.

The arrangement of each entry is consistent, for books being:
Title
Author
Publisher
Date
Number of pages
and for periodical articles:
Title
Author (if quoted in article)
Title of periodical
Volume number
Date of issue
Page numbers of article

In certain cases, footnotes are included in order to explain the title or coverage.

In general, the following have been omitted from the bibliography:
Periodical articles of one page or less, unless the content is of outstanding importance or the subject has received little coverage
Periodical articles in "non-transport" or engineering journals unless the subject is little-documented
Topographical works containing general information on tramways
Guide books and maps produced by individual tramway systems
Rule books belonging to individual systems
Works of fiction containing tramway references

To obtain copies of any of the items contained in this bibliography, you should enquire at your local public library. If the item is not in stock, the library should be able to borrow a copy from another library via the regional inter-lending scheme. Copies of most of the periodical articles can also be obtained in the same way. Alternatively, you may be able to consult any book/article at the National Tramway Museum Library at Crich, though an appointment may be necessary to do so. Much of the less obscure material can also be obtained second-hand from Adam Gordon, whose address will be found behind the title page.

We are most grateful to Richard Wiseman for checking the final text.

And finally, if you spot the omission of a significant book or periodical article, please let us know, so that we can keep our coverage as comprehensive as possible.

David Croft, Bradford, October 2003

HISTORICAL INTRODUCTION

The region covered by this source book is one of marked contrasts. Its population spreads from Carlisle in the north through the beautiful Lake District, to the mill towns of East Lancashire, and westwards again to the seaside resorts of Blackpool and Morecambe. Because of the geographical nature of the area, there are clusters of population, and tramways played an important part of everyday life, whether serving mill-workers and holidaymakers alike.

As in many other parts of the country, the horse tram appeared on the scene in the 1870's and 1880's but was soon to be joined by the steam tram, but both were soon superseded by the electric tram which was seen as the way forward. However, this region was also notable in seeing other forms of tramcar propulsion, with gas trams at Lytham St. Anne's, and later still, petrol-driven trams at Morecambe.

Many of the tramway systems in the area were only small and had a short life, and during the 1930's most were replaced entirely by motor buses – no trolley bus replacements featured in this part of the country. Morecambe was notable in that it retained its horse trams until 1926, and was the last horse tram system to survive on the English mainland.

There was of course one tramway system in the north-west which continued to develop and prosper – Blackpool. Right from its inception, the Blackpool tramway developed like no other system, with high-capacity "Dreadnought" cars and circular tours which captured the imagination of the visitors and became an important part of a holiday in the resort. Then in 1933 came Walter Luff as the new General Manager. Within a very short time there was a revolutionary new fleet of streamlined trams which still form the back-bone of the fleet seventy years later. Although the town services were abandoned, still the system developed with modern trailer cars, new illuminated feature cars, and in more recent times both double and single deck one-person operated trams, resulting in the Blackpool tramway system being a tourist attraction in its own right. It may yet see further development which turns it into the area's first light rail system, with the added attraction of retaining heritage trams along the promenade.

Many of the systems in the area took advantage of purchasing second-hand trams to keep their systems going – Barrow, Preston and Lytham St. Anne's being examples.

Several ambitious tramway plans would have added considerable attraction to this area had they been built. At the turn of the last century, plans were drawn up for a tramway between Lytham St. Anne's and Southport using a transporter bridge to carry trams across the estuary of the river Ribble. Around the same time were schemes for a tramway system based around Windermere and Bowness in the Lake District which, could have been a great success in this area of outstanding natural beauty, though a lengthy standard gauge line on the Cumbrian coast might have proved a little too ambitious.

The area could also boast two tramcar construction plants. The Lancaster Carriage & Wagon Company built cars for the Lancaster, Morecambe and Blackpool systems, whilst the Electric Railway & Tramway Carriage Works which opened in Preston in 1898, were to supply many of the country's tramcars under various names over the years, including Dick, Kerr & Company, the United Electric Car Company and later as part of the English Electric empire.

In other parts of the country, plans for the return of the tram are progressing, though it is doubtful that North Lancashire will see such developments. However, Blackpool is still awaiting the outcome of a bid for government money to fund a modernised system in the resort, but even if approved it could be many years before a new tramway is born.

CHRONOLOGY OF TRAMWAYS OF NORTH LANCASHIRE & CUMBRIA

1879   Preston Tramways Company began operating horse trams in the town.

1880   Proposals for a horse tramway from the Blackpool boundary to St. Anne's and Lytham came to nothing.

1881   Blackburn & Over Darwen Tramways Company began operating steam trams.
Burnley and District Tramways Company commenced steam tram operation.

1882   Preston Corporation began running horse trams.

1885   Morecambe Tramways Company formed to establish tramways in the resort.
Steam trams commenced in Barrow-in-Furness.
Blackpool Electric Tramway Company inaugurated the country's first electric street tramway using the conduit system.

1886   Accrington Corporation Steam Tramways Company inaugurated tramways.

1887   Horse tramways opened along Morecambe Promenade.
Steam trams introduced by the Blackburn Corporation Tramways Co. Ltd.

1888   Lancaster & District Tramways Company formed to operate horse trams between Lancaster and Morecambe which opened in 1890.

1889   Rossendale Valley Tramways Company began operating steam trams between Bacup and Rawtenstall.

1892   Blackpool Electric Tramway Company acquired by Blackpool Corporation.

1893   Blackpool, St. Anne's & Lytham Tramways Company formed to take over the 1880 horse tram scheme.

1896   Blackpool, St. Anne's & Lytham Tramways Company began operating gas trams leased to the British Gas Traction Company.

1897   Blackburn Corporation Tramways Co. Ltd.

1898   Barrow steam tram company goes into liquidation but steam trams continued to run intermittently until 1903.
Blackpool & Fleetwood Tramroad Company opened its electric tramway along the coast.

Carlisle Tramways Order granted the establishment of a small tramway network in the city.

Blackpool, St. Anne's & Lytham Tramways Company formed to take over the gas trams.

Electric Railway & Tramway Carriage Works Ltd. established a tramcar building factory in Preston.

Plans to build a tramway between Lytham and Southport across the Ribble estuary failed to receive Parliamentary approval.

1899 British Electric Traction Company acquired the Barrow steam trams with plans to electrify the system.

Proposals for an electric tramway from Bowness and Windermere to Grasmere were discussed.

Electric trams introduced by Blackburn Corporation following the take-over of the Blackburn and Over Darwen and Blackburn Tramways companies.

Blackpool Corporation converted their lines from conduit operation to overhead wire current collection.

1900 City of Carlisle Electric Tramways Company commenced operation.

Darwen Corporation began operating electric trams.

Rossendale Valley Tramways Company was acquired by the British Electric Traction Company.

Burnley Corporation acquired the steam tram operations of the Burnley & District Tramways Co.

1901 Blackpool, St. Anne's & Lytham Tramways Company was acquired by the Electric Tramways Construction & Maintenance Company, and was itself soon purchased by Blackpool Electric Tramways (South) Ltd.

Blackpool & Garstang Light Railway obtained powers to build a tramway between the two towns.

Burnley Corporation introduced electric trams.

Powers were granted for a 31 miles standard gauge tramway along the Cumberland coast, but it was never built.

1903 Preston Tramways Company horse trams ceased.

Electric trams commenced operation between Blackpool, St. Anne's and Lytham.

Opening of Lancaster Corporation's electric tramway system.

Nelson Corporation introduced electric trams.

	Colne and Trawden Light Railway opened.
1904	Electric trams introduced by Preston Corporation. British Electric Traction Company began running electric trams in Barrow-in-Furness.
1907	Accrington Corporation acquired the company-owned steam trams and introduced electric trams.
1908	Haslingden Corporation acquired a short section of line from the Accrington Corporation Steam Tramways Company which was later electrified and worked by Accrington Corporation.
1909	Morecambe Corporation acquired part of the town's horse tram network. Rawtenstall Corporation electrified the former Rossendale Valley Tramways Company steam tram route.
1911	Balfour Beatty Group acquired the Carlisle tramway operations.
1912	Morecambe Tramways Company purchased four petrol trams for use on its short route. First Blackpool illuminated tram introduced.
1914	Colne Corporation acquired the Colne and Trawden Light Railway Company and adopted the title "Colne Corporation Light Railways".
1920	St. Anne's Urban District Council acquired the electric tramways in St. Anne's and Lytham. Blackpool Corporation acquired the Blackpool & Fleetwood Tramroad Company. Barrow Corporation acquired the electric tramway in the town from the British Electric Traction Company.
1921	Abortive attempt made to revive plans for a tramway from Bowness to Grasmere with an extension to Keswick. Lancaster to Morecambe horse trams ceased.
1922	St. Anne's Urban District Council became Lytham St. Anne's Corporation on amalgamation of the two boroughs.
1924	Morecambe Tramways Company petrol trams scrapped and replaced by motor buses.
1926	Morecambe Corporation horse trams replaced by motor buses. Lytham St. Anne's Corporation trams began running through Blackpool to Gynn Square. Morecambe Tramways Company went into liquidation with their bus operations being taken over by Heysham & District Motors.

1928	Lytham St. Anne's Corporation trams began running on Blackpool's New South Promenade.
1930	Lancaster Corporation trams replaced by motor buses.
1931	Carlisle trams replaced by United and Ribble buses.
1932	Closure of Rawtenstall Corporation tramway system. Barrow Corporation trams replaced by motor buses. Motor buses replaced Accrington Corporation trams.
1933	Burnley, Colne and Nelson Joint Transport established, acquiring the trams of all three towns.
1934	Colne Corporation Light Railways and Nelson Corporation trams replaced by buses of Burnley, Colne and Nelson Joint Transport.
1935	Burnley tramway system closed. Preston Corporation trams replaced by motor buses.
1936	Trams ceased to operate between St. Anne's and Lytham.
1937	Lytham St. Anne's Corporation replaced the remainder of its trams with motor buses.
1946	Darwen Corporation trams replaced by buses.
1949	Closure of Blackburn Corporation tramway system.
1958	First trailer car introduced at Blackpool.
1963	Last of Blackpool's inland tram services replaced by buses.
1972	One-man operated single deck trams introduced at Blackpool.
1985	Centenary of Blackpool tramway system.
1991	Construction of new tramway on Blackpool's North Pier.

CLASSIFICATION SCHEME

A   General works

B   Specific tramway systems

        Accrington Corporation Tramways

        Barrow-in-Furness Tramways

        Blackburn Corporation Tramways

        Blackpool Corporation Tramways; Blackpool and Fleetwood Tramroad Company; Blackpool, St. Anne's & Lytham Tramways Company, and Lytham St. Anne's Corporation Tramways

        Burnley Corporation Tramways

        City of Carlisle Electric Tramways Company

        Colne Tramways

        Darwen Corporation Tramways

        Haslingden Corporation Tramways

        Lancaster Tramways

        Morecambe Tramways

        Nelson Corporation Tramways

        Preston Corporation Tramways

        Rawtenstall Corporation Tramways

C   Works on other tramways

        Blackpool North Pier Tramway

D   Light Rail schemes

E   Tramway museums and preservation

F   Tramway Manufacturers

G   Reference material

        1   Books

        2   Periodicals

        3   Newspapers

        4   Legislation

        5   Accident reports

        6   Timetables and guides

        7   Maps

        8   Council minutes

        9   Annual reports

        10   Trade literature

        11   Arbitration/litigation/law reports

H   Library addresses

Publishing programme

A. GENERAL WORKS

Great British Tramway Networks. BETT, W.H & GILLHAM, J.C. Light Railway Transport League: 1st ed. 1940, 85pp; 2nd ed. 1944, 96pp; 3rd ed. 1957, 224pp; 4th ed. 1962, 220pp.

The Golden Age of Tramways. KLAPPER, C. Routledge & Kegan Paul: lst ed. 1961, 327pp; 2nd ed. David & Charles, 1974, 327pp.

Blackpool Journey. EVANS, M. *Trams* No.23, October 1966, pp.4-8. (A journey across Lancashire).

The lights go out in Lancashire. EVANS, M. In Tramway Memories. JOYCE, J. (ed.), Ian Allan, 1967, pp.109-124, (Reminiscences of various Lancashire systems).

Crossing the Ribble. BOND, A.W. *Modern Tramway*, vol.32, no.379, July 1969, pp.234-240. (Abortive schemes of 1899-1906 for a crossing between Southport and Lytham by tram).

Over the setts: East Lancashire trams and buses. CATLOW, R. & COLLINGE, Tom. Countryside Publications Ltd., 1978, 48pp.

Development of Lancashire's trams and buses, Part 1. South-eastern area – Hyndburn and Rossendale, 75 years of Municipal operation. DEEGAN, P. Omnibus Society, 1982, 36pp.

Tramways of North Lancashire. BETT, W.H. & GILLHAM, J.C. edited by PRICE, J.H. Light Rail Transit Association, 1985, 68pp.

Travelling around the Fylde: a picture postcard viewpoint. DEEGAN, J. and DEEGAN, P, Communications, 1989, 58pp.

Trams in the North-West. HESKETH, P. Ian Allan, 1995, 128pp.

Circular Tour: seaside pleasure riding by tram. TURNER, B. Rio Vista 1999 (Includes Blackpool, Lytham, Southport and Morecambe).

Circular Tour: seaside pleasure riding by tram. TURNER, B. Rio Vista, 1999 (includes Blackpool, Lytham, Southport and Morecambe).

B. WORKS ON SPECIFIC TRAMWAY SYSTEMS

ACCRINGTON CORPORATION TRAMWAYS

Accrington Corporation Tramways: a converted and extended system. *Light Railway & Tramway Journal*, vol.17, 1 November 1907, pp.304-308.

The Accrington Corporation Tramways. RUSH, R.W. *Modern Tramway*, vol.6, no.68, August 1943, pp.61/65/67-68.

Accrington electrifies. MARSHALL, D.R. *Omnibus Magazine*, October 1957, pp.111-112.

The tramways of Accrington, 1886-1932, with brief notes on the adjoining systems of Blackburn, Darwen, Haslingden, and Rawtenstall. RUSH, R.W. Light Railway Transport League, 1961, 88pp.

Tramway treasury – a pictorial history of Accrington and District Tramways, 1886-1932. DAWSON, T. 1975, 64pp.

Accrington's public transport, 1886-1986. RUSH, R.W. Landy Publishing, 2000, 60pp.

BARROW-IN-FURNESS TRAMWAYS

Barrow-in-Furness Tramways. *Light Railway & Tramway Journal*, vol.10, 6 May 1904, pp.339-342.

The tramways of Barrow-in-Furness. *Tramway & Railway World*, vol.16, 11 August 1904, pp.129-134.

Progress in the use of trail cars: Barrow adopts type of car used in London. *Tramway & Railway World*, vol.42, 18 October 1917, pp.233-234.

Seventy-five years on wheels: the history of public transport in Barrow-in-Furness, 1885-1960. CORMACK, I.L. Scottish Tramway Museum Society, 1960, 56pp.

Transport of Barrow-in-Furness: ninety years on wheels. CORMACK, I.L. 1974, 14pp.

Barrow-in-Furness transport: a century on wheels. CORMACK, I.L. 1977, 17pp, 24pp.

BLACKBURN CORPORATION TRAMWAYS

The Blackburn and Darwen tramways. FORBES, N.N. *Modern Tramway,* vol.5, no.58, October 1942, p.91; vol.5, no.59, November 1942, p.102; vol.5, no.60, December 1942, pp.112-113.

Farewell to Blackburn's trams. Blackburn Corporation Tramways, 1949, 20pp.

The tramways of Accrington, 1886-1932, with brief notes on the adjoining systems of Blackburn, Darwen, Haslingden, and Rawtenstall. RUSH, R.W. Light Railway Transport League, 1961, 88pp.

Meeting Blackburn's trams. YEARSLEY, I. *Modern Tramway,* vol.29, no.345, September 1966, pp.309-316.

British trams in camera. THOMPSON, J. Ian Allan, 1978, 128pp (Blackburn, pp.80-81).

The first in the kingdom: a history of buses and trams in Blackburn and Darwen. FERGUSSON, R.P. & OTHERS. Darwen Transport Group, 1981, 56pp.

British and Irish tramway systems since 1945. WALLER, M.H & WALLER, P. Ian Allan, 1992, 192pp (Blackburn, pp.29-31).

Blackburn tram rides. HALSALL, J. Landy Publishing, 1999, 60pp.

BLACKPOOL CORPORATION TRAMWAYS; THE BLACKPOOL AND FLEETWOOD TRAMROAD COMPANY; BLACKPOOL, ST.ANNE'S & LYTHAM TRAMWAYS COMPANY, AND LYTHAM ST.ANNE'S CORPORATION TRAMWAYS.

[Because of the complexities of ownership, track-sharing and take-overs, plus the fact that much of the literature refers to more than one system, it has been decided to combine the above four systems into one section].

The Blackpool Electric Tramways. *Engineer,* vol.61, 1 January 1886, pp.4-6.

The Blackpool electric tramway. SMITH, M.H. 1887, 33pp. (A paper read before the British Association at Birmingham).

The Blackpool electric tramway. *Tramway & Railway World,* vol.1, October 1892, pp.375-378.

Gas motor tram cars for Blackpool, St. Anne's and Lytham tramways. *Engineer,* vol.82, 17 July 1896, pp.66-67.

The Blackpool and Fleetwood Electric Tramroad. *Railway World,* vol.7, 8 September 1898, pp.279-289.

The tramways of Blackpool and neighbourhood. *Railway World,* vol.7, 8 December 1898, pp.409-410.

Blackpool, St. Anne's and Lytham Tramways. *Light Railway & Tramway Journal,* vol.11, 4 November 1904, pp.337-339.

Blackpool, St. Anne's and Lytham Tramways Co. Ltd. *Railway World,* vol.19, 7 June 1906, pp.537-540.

Blackpool Corporation Tramways and the Blackpool & Fleetwood and Blackpool, St. Anne's & Lytham Tramways. *Electric Railway & Tramway Journal,* vol.37, 7 September 1917, pp.85-92.

Blackpool Corporation. Tramways v. Buses. *Journal of the Municipal Tramways Association,* 1922, pp.487-488.

New cars for Lytham St. Anne's Corporation Tramways. *Tramway & Railway World,* vol.55, 20 March 1924, pp.125-128.

New tramcars for Blackpool Corporation. *Tramway & Railway World,* vol.64, 18 October 1928, pp.209-212.

New tramcars for Blackpool Corporation. *Electric Railway & Tramway Journal,* vol.59, 9 November 1928, pp.326-328.

Progress: the new Blackpool tramcar. *Electric Railway, Bus & Tram Journal,* vol.68, 23 June 1933, pp.329-334.

Blackpool's new single deck car. *Tramway & Railway World,* vol.74, 13 July 1933, pp.9-14.

Blackpool tramways new rolling stock. *Transport World,* vol.76, 8 November 1934, pp.235-239.

New tramcars for Blackpool. *Electric Railway, Bus & Tram Journal,* vol.71, 9 November 1934, pp.527-530.

Blackpool Tramways new rolling stock. *Omnibus Magazine,* vol.6, June 1935, pp.42-43.

Serving a huge holidaymaking public. *Omnibus Magazine,* vol.6, December 1935, pp.73-74 (The Blackpool tramway system).

Blackpool's latest luxury tramcars. *Transport World,* vol.82, 12 August 1937, pp.110-112.

Blackpool's latest type of railcoach. *Passenger Transport Journal,* vol.77, 13 August 1937, pp.70-71.

The new rail-coaches for Blackpool: details of the electrical equipment. *Passenger Transport Journal*, vol.77, 12 November 1937, pp.268-270.

Fifty years of progress at Blackpool. *Transport World*, vol.85, 11 May 1939, pp.245-248.

A tale of three trams: sea breezes and modern cars on the Lancashire coast. *Modern Tramway*, vol.2, no.19, July 1939, pp.76/78. (Blackpool rolling stock).

A history of the Blackpool tramways. HENSON, J.R. *Modern Tramway*, vol.12, no.136, April 1949, pp.69/80-86.

Modern transport by tramcar. *Passenger Transport Journal*, vol.105, 15 August 1951, pp.273-274/276 (Description of the Blackpool 'Coronation' cars).

Blackpool's growing tram fleet. *Transport World*, vol.112, 5 July 1952, pp.19-20. (Description of the 'Coronation' cars).

Latest Blackpool railcars. *Passenger Transport Journal*, vol.107, 9 July 1952, pp.75-76/78.

When Blackpool lights up. PRICE, J.H. *Modern Tramway*, vol.16, no.185, May 1953, pp.90-92 (Story of Blackpool's illuminated cars).

The tramways of Lytham St. Anne's. PHILLIPS, D.F. *Tramway Review*, vol.2, no.14, 1954, pp.106-125; vol.3, no.24, 1958, p.190.

Progress at Blackpool. *Transport World*, vol.115, 1 May 1954, pp.462-463 (Description of the Blackpool system).

From Blackpool to Fleetwood by Tramroad. PHILLIPS, D.F. *Railway Magazine*, vol.101, no.653, September 1955, pp.641-645.

The television twins. PRICE, J.H. *Modern Tramway*, vol.19, no.227, November 1956, pp.191-195 (Story of Blackpool's television cars 165/166).

The conduit tramways of Blackpool, 1885-1899. PHILLIPS, D.F. *Tramway Review*, vol.3, no.21, 1956, pp.108-119; vol.3, nos.22/23, 1957, pp.122-123.

The tram that went to America. PHILLIPS, D.F. & PEARSON, F.K. Light Railway Transport League, 1958, 16pp (Account of Blackpool car 144's journey to America, and description of the Blackpool system).

The Blackpool & Fleetwood Tramroad Company, 1896-1920. PHILLIPS, D.F. *Tramway Review*, vol.4, no.25, 1958, pp.2-29.

Progress at Blackpool: trailer unit enters service. PRICE, J.H. *Modern Tramway*, vol.21, no.246, June 1958, pp.129-134.

Blackpool's diesel tramcar. PRICE, J.H. *Modern Tramway*, vol.21, no.250, October 1958, pp.223-224. (Story of Blackpool works car no.3).

Tramways of Lytham St. Anne's. ABELL, P.H & OTHERS. Oakwood Press, 1995, 128pp.

The Blackpool Belle. PALMER, G.S. *Modern Tramway*, vol. 22, no.263, November 1959, pp.213-215 (Story of an illuminated tram).

75 years of electric street tramway operation. COUNTY BOROUGH OF BLACKPOOL. 1960, 13pp.

Blackpool tram fleet survey, April 1960. PALMER, G.S. *Blackpool Tramway News,* 1960, 6pp.

Blackpool Corporation Tramways. PHILLIPS, D.F. *Tramway Review,* vol.4, no.28, 1960, pp.90-119.

75 years of Blackpool progress. PHILLIPS, D.F & PALMER, G.S. *Modern Tramway*, vol.23, no.273, September 1960, pp.204-210.

The new Blackpool trailer cars. THOMAS, G.R. *Modern Tramway,* vol.23, no.273, September 1960, pp.211-213.

Blackpool's old soldiers. PRICE, J.H. *Modern Tramway*, vol.23, no.273, September 1960, pp.214-218 (Blackpool's vintage trams).

The Blackpool trailer trucks. THOMAS, G.R. *Modern Tramway,* vol.24, no.284, August 1961, pp.220-221.

Blackpool, Summer 1961. TERRY, A.K. & PRICE, J.H. *Modern Tramway,* vol.24, no.287, November 1961, pp.315-320. (General description of the system).

Blackpool prepares for the 1962 season. TERRY, A.K. *Modern Tramway*, vol.25, no.296, August 1962, pp.258-260.

Wild west tramniks. PRICE, J.H. *Modern Tramway*, vol.25, no.298, October 1962, pp.340-346 (Blackpool's illuminated trams).

Blackpool 167. PACKER, A.D. *Trams*, no.7, October 1962, pp.4-7.

North Station and Fleetwood, 1897-1963. PALMER, G.S. Blackpool & Fylde Tramway Historical Association, 1963, 16pp.

The Marton experiment. PEARSON, F.K. *Modern Tramway*, vol.26, no.301, January 1963, pp.14-19; vol.26, no.302, February 1963, pp.51-56 (Developments on the Marton route in Blackpool).

Retrospect and prospect: a decade of Blackpool tramways, 1955-1965. PALMER, G.S. In **Modern Tramway Review.** ed. JOYCE, J. Ian Allan, 1964, pp.5-18.

Blackpool 167. PRICE, J.H. *Modern Tramway*, vol.27, no. 315, March 1964, pp.81-84.

Watch the birdie! PRICE, J.H. *Modern Tramway*, vol.27, no.318, June 1964, pp.204-207 (Blackpool tramway photographic trips in the early 1900's).

By tram to the Tower: 80 years of Blackpool tramways. PALMER, G.S. 1968, 68pp.

Behind the scenes at Blackpool: a major re-organisation. PALMER, G.S. *Modern Tramway*, vol.28, no.326, February 1965, pp.36-44; vol.28, no.327, March 1965, pp.76-81.

Our trams 1: Fleetwood 40. PALMER, G.S. *Tramway Museum Society Journal*, vol.6, no.25, April 1965, pp.28-31, 34-36.

H.M.S. Blackpool. PRICE, J.H. *Modern Tramway*, vol.28, no.334, October 1965, pp.324-326 (Story of an illuminated tram).

The £.s.d. of Blackpool's trams. PRICE, J.H *Modern Tramway*, vol.29, no.339, March 1966, pp.78-87.

The plastic tram. TURNER, B. *Modern Tramway*, vol.29, no.340, April 1966, pp.114-116 (The rebuilding of Blackpool car 264).

Blackpool night out. TURNER, B. *Modern Tramway*, vol.29, no.346, October 1966, pp.331-334 (Night maintenance on the Blackpool tramway system).

Blackpool Corporation Transport. DOUGILL, D.A. *Buses Illustrated*, vol.17, no.150, September 1967, pp.359-367/375; vol.17, no.152, November 1967, pp.452-461/465.

Blackpool by tram. PALMER, G.S. & TURNER, B.R. 1968, 100pp.

Sixes and sevens. TURNER, B. *Modern Tramway*, vol.31, no.367, July 1968, pp.226-228 (The renumbering of the Blackpool tram fleet).

A note on the Blackpool conduit cars. DOUGILL, D.A. *Tramway Review* Vol.7, No.54, Summer 1968, pp.136-141.

The stop past Central. WARDLE, R.S. *Modern Tramway*, vol.34, No.399, March 1971, pp.91-99 (Reminiscences of a summer conductor at Blackpool).

Could Blackpool go one-man? PRICE, J.H. *Modern Tramway*, vol.34, no.405, September 1971, pp.300-308.

Always a tram in sight: a picture history of Blackpool's trams. MACKENZIE, J. Light Railway Transport League, 1972, 60pp.

Blackpool's new one-man trams. MACKENZIE, J. *Modern Tramway*, vol.35, no.414, June 1972, pp.195-197.

Blackpool 166. TERRY, A.K. *Journal of the Tramway Museum Society*, vol.11, no.61, July 1972, pp.10-11.

The Blackpool toastracks. TURNER, B.R. *Modern Tramway*, vol.36, no.429, September 1973, pp.295-302.
Edwardian Blackpool – a tour by tram with excursions to Fleetwood and Lytham. PALMER, G.S. & TURNER, B.R. 1974, 28pp.
Blackpool 166. TERRY, A.K. *Journal of the Tramway Museum Society*, vol.14, no.72, April 1975, pp.36-39; vol.14, no.73, July 1975, pp.64-66.
Blackpool: a tradition of trams. GARNHAM, J.A. 1976, 48pp.
The Blackpool story. TURNER, B.R & PALMER, G.S. 1976, 140pp. (Social history of Blackpool with many references to the trams).
British trams in camera. THOMPSON, J. Ian Allan, 1978, 128pp (Blackpool pp.82-89).
Blackpool by tram. PALMER, G. S. & TURNER, R. Transport Publishing Co., 1978, 112pp.
Blackpool to Fleetwood. TURNER, B. Light Railway Transport League, c.1978, 99pp.
Blackpool goes one-man. PALMER, G. S. *Modern Tramway*, vol.41, no.483, March 1978, pp.74-80; vol.41, no.484, April 1978, pp.116-121.
Not forgotten. KING, B. *Journal of the Tramway Museum Society*, vol.18, no.88, April 1979, pp.33-36 (Story of Blackpool car 167).
New Blackpool double-deck car enters service. TUDOR, D. *Modern Tramway*, vol.42, no.502, October 1979, pp.353-358.
Blackpool 761 – Balloon resurgam. ABELL, P.H. *Journal of the Tramway Museum Society*, vol.18, no.90, October 1979, pp.90-91.
Sampling Britain's newest tramcar. WAYMAN, D. *Fare Stage*, vol.2, no.4, December 1979/January 1980, pp.118-119 (Story of Blackpool car 761).
Obituary of J.C.Franklin (1910-1980), (former Manager of Blackpool Corporation Tramways. *Modern Tramway*, vol.43, no.508, April 1980, pp.141-142.
Blackpool by tram. PALMER, S & TURNER, B. Authors in association with Transport Publishing Co., 3rd ed. 1981, 112pp.
The Blackpool tramway. TRAMWAY MUSEUM SOCIETY. 1981, 32pp.
Trams and buses around Blackpool. PALMER, S & TURNER, B Authors, 80pp.
A night at the lights. PRICE, J.H. *Modern Tramway*, vol.45, no.536, August 1982, pp.310-315 (Blackpool's illuminated tramcars).

Progress at Blackpool. WYSE, W.J. *Modern Tramway*, vol.46, no.543, March 1983, pp.74-79 (Developments at Blackpool, 1982-1983).

The new Blackpool tram. (Car 641). HYDE, D.L. In: **Electrifying urban public transport.** LESLEY, L (ed). Liverpool Polytechnic, 1984, pp.57-63.

Progress towards the centenary at Blackpool. PALMER, S. *Modern Tramway*, vol.47, no.556, April 1984, pp.115-117.

The Blackpool steeplecab locomotive. TERRY, K. *Journal of the Tramway Museum Society,* vol.23, no.108, October 1984, pp.77-78.

A centenary celebration of Blackpool's trams. HIGGS, P. Lancastrian Transport Publications, 1985, 120pp.

Blackpool's new tramcars – the modernisation of the Blackpool tram fleet. HYDE, D.L. Tramway Museum Society, 1985, 24pp.

Blackpool's trams. JOYCE, J. Ian Allan, 1985, 48pp.

Blackpool's century of trams. PALMER, S. Blackpool Borough Council, 1985, 112pp.

Innovation and survival: the story of the Blackpool tramway 1885-1985. PALMER, G.S. Tramway & Light Railway Society, 1985, 32pp (Walter Gratwicke Memorial Lecture, 1985).

Blackpool 641. WYSE, W.J. *Modern Tramway*, vol.48, no.565, January 1985, pp.12-15; vol.48, no.566, February 1985, pp.38-42.

Blackpool's tramway centenary. CLAYDON, G.B. *Modern Tramway*, vol.48, no.566, February 1985, pp.44-45.

Blackpool 651. CLAYDON, G.B. *Modern Tramway*, vol.48, no.574, October 1985, pp.337-340.

Blackpool centenary celebrations get under way. CLAYDON, G.B. *Modern Tramway*, vol.48, no.574, October 1985, pp.342-345.

Fleetbook of Blackpool's trams. HIGGS, P. Lancastrian Transport Publications, 1986, 24pp.

Trams in Blackpool. JOHNSON, P. AB Publishing, 1986, 48pp (Survey of Centenary year, 1985).

Classic tramcars. WISEMAN, R.J.S. Ian Allan, 1986, 128pp (Blackpool, pp.131-136).

Being a steam tram of uncertain temperament. TEBB, R. *Journal of the Tramway Museum Society,* vol.25, no.113, January 1986, pp.10-16 (Story of locomotive 'John Bull's visit to Blackpool).

The Blackpool centenary: climax and finale. CLAYDON, G.B. *Modern Tramway*, vol.49, no.578, February 1986, pp.51-60.

Blackpool celebrates 100 years of electric trams. PORTER, A.F. *Vintage Roadscene*, vol.2, no.6, March-May 1986, pp.46-47.

Blackpool and Fleetwood by tram. PALMER, S. Platform 5 Publications, 1988, 96pp.

Summerhouse 619. PRICE J.H. *Modern Tramway*, vol.51, no.600, June 1988, pp.209-211 (New Blackpool car 619).

Derek Hyde retires. DEPLEDGE, A. *Modern Tramway*, vol.52, no.616, April 1989, pp.115-117 (Former Blackpool tramway manager).

Trams to the Tower. PALMER, S & HIGGS, P. Lancastrian Transport Publications, 1990, 56pp (A review of the 1990 tram fleet).

The phoenix arises. PILLAR, S. In: **Supertram**. WALLER, P. Ian Allan, 1990, pp.20-23/26-27 (The modernisation of Blackpool's tramways).

Blackpool's tram fleet. PRICE, J.H. *Modern Tramway*, vol.53, no.630, June 1990, pp.190-192 (Review of current fleet).

A tale of two tramcars. PALMER, S. *Journal of the Tramway Museum Society*, vol.29, no.131, July 1990, pp.65-67 (Aspects of Blackpool tramcar preservation).

Fleetbook of Blackpool Transport trams and buses. PENNEY, M. Lancastrian Transport Publications, 1991, 28pp.

British & Irish tramway systems since 1945. WALLER, M.H & P. Ian Allan, 1992, 192pp (Blackpool pp.32-39).

Tramride to Fleetwood. MARTIN, B.P. *Tramfare*, no.147, May-June 1992, pp.10-14.

The classic trams. WALLER, P. Ian Allan, 1993, 128pp (Blackpool Standards, pp.7-14; Blackpool Streamliners, pp.43-60).

Blackpool & Fleetwood 40: the last 12 years. HYDE, S & BROOMFIELD, S. *Journal of the Tramway Museum Society*, vol.32, no.141, January 1993, pp.18-21.

Stan "The Tram" Croasdale: the memories of a transport man. WILSON, M. Lancastrian Transport Publications, 1994, 30pp (Recollections of a Blackpool tram man).

Current progress in Blackpool. PALMER, S. In: *Light Rail Review 6*. Platform 5 Publishing, 1994, pp.13-15.

The Blackpool tramway in winter. BERRY, E. Lancastrian Transport Publications, 1995, 44pp.

Tramways of Lytham St. Anne's. ABELL, P.H. & OTHERS. Oakwood Press, 1995, 128pp.

A nostalgic look at Blackpool trams 1950-1966. PALMER, S. Silver Link Publishing, 1995, 100pp.

Blackpool, 1995. KIRKMAN, A. *Tramfare*, no.167, September-October 1995, pp.2-8.

The wall of death. ROBINSON, B. *Vintage Roadscene*, vol.11, no.44, September-November 1995, pp.157-160 (Recollections of driving Blackpool trams).

Blackpool looks forward. *Light Rail & Modern Tramway*, vol.58, no.695, November 1995, Supplement i-viii.

Heyday of Blackpool's trams. PALMER, S. Ian Allan, 1996, 80pp.

Blackpool trams: the first half century, 1885-1932. ABELL, P.H. & McLOUGHLIN, I. Oakwood Press, 1997, 224pp.

Blackpool and Fleetwood: 100 years by tram. PALMER, S. Platform 5 Publishing, 1998, 143pp.

Blackpool: making easier access affordable. HIGGS, P. *Tramways & Urban Transit*, vol.61, no.726, June 1998, pp.218-219.

100 years of Blackpool & Fleetwood 2. BEARDSELL, D. *Journal of the Tramway Museum Society*, vol.37, no.163, July 1998, pp.98-104.

Blackpool's carbuncle tram – 707. RAMSDEN, S. *Fylde Tramway News*, no.217, September 1998, pp.6-7.

The second century. BEARDSELL, D. *Journal of the Tramway Museum Society*, vol.37, no.164, October 1998, pp.144-146 (Blackpool & Fleetwood 2).

100 years of trams in Fleetwood. SLATER, M. *Vintage Roadscene*, vol.15, no.57, December1998-February 1999, pp.22-25.

Highlights of Blackpool's trams. PALMER, S. Tramroad House, 2001, 72pp.

Blackpool's OMO cars. HIGGS, P. Lancastrian Transport Publications, 2002, 32pp (Deals with first generation cars 1-13).

Dreadnought 59 – now a centenarian. PALMER, S. *Journal of the Tramway Museum Society*, vol.41, no.177, January 2002, pp.14-18.

BURNLEY CORPORATION TRAMWAYS

New rolling stock on the Burnley tramways. *Railway World*, vol.6, June 1897, pp.178-179.

Burnley Corporation electric tramways. *Tramway & Railway World*, vol.11, 17 April 1902, pp.199-210.

Burnley Corporation Tramways. MOZLEY, H. *Light Railway & Tramway Journal,* vol.11, 2 December 1904, pp.422-424.
Burnley tramways depot. MOZLEY, H. *Tramway & Railway World,* vol.18, 9 November 1905, pp.446-450.
Burnley Corporation Tramways. MOZLEY, H. *Tramway & Railway World,* vol.18, 7 December 1905, pp.569-574.
New design of top-covered vestibule car for Burnley Corporation Tramways. MOZLEY, H. *Tramway & Railway World,* vol.25, 3 June 1909, pp.437-438.
Recent new equipments at Burnley. MOZLEY, H. *Tramway & Railway World,* vol.31, 11 January 1912, pp.24-25.
Burnley district transport. LEE, C.E. *Omnibus Magazine,* vol.4, no.40, April 1933, pp.85-88.
British tramways recalled: Burnley-Nelson-Colne-Preston. *Trams,* no.23, October 1966, pp.15-19.
Memories of Burnley trams. SMITH, K.H. *Modern Tramway,* vol.31, no.366, June 1968, pp.185-195.
The Burnley tramways centenary. HARRISON, M. *Journal of the Tramway Museum Society,* vol.21, no.99, January 1982, pp.14-17.
Burnley steam trams: on trial, on gradients & in song. HARRISON, M. *Tramway Review,* vol.20, no.155, Autumn 1993, pp.113-116.
The tram restored at Burnley. HARRISON, M. *Tramway Review,* vol.21, no.168, Winter 1996, pp.284-305; vol.21, no.169, Spring 1997, pp.4-23.

CITY OF CARLISLE ELECTRIC TRAMWAYS COMPANY
City of Carlisle electric tramways. *Railway World,* vol.9, 11 October 1900, pp.477-484.
Tramways of the City of Carlisle. HEARSE, G.S. Author, 1962, 52pp.
Tramways in the City of Carlisle. HEARSE, G.S. Author, 1978, 52pp.

COLNE TRAMWAYS
British tramways recalled: Burnley-Nelson-Colne-Preston. *Trams,* no.23, October 1966, pp.15-19.
The light railways of Colne. KING, J.S. *Tramway Review,* vol.9, no.72, Winter 1972, pp.227-233/239-242; vol.9, no.73, Spring 1973, pp.259-274; vol.10, no.74, Summer 1973, pp.50-62.

DARWEN CORPORATION TRAMWAYS
Darwen electric tramways and refuse destructor. *Tramway & Railway World,* vol.10, 7 February 1901, pp.60-71.

Darwen low-type bogie tramcars. *Electric Railway & Tramway Journal,* vol.52, 13 February 1925, pp.61-62.

The Blackburn and Darwen tramways. FORBES, N.N. *Modern Tramway,* vol.5, no. 58, October 1942, p.91; vol.5, no.59, November 1942, p.102; vol.5, no.60, December 1942, pp.112-113.

Souvenir of the abandonment of tramways, 5th October 1946. BOROUGH OF DARWEN TRANSPORT DEPARTMENT. 1946, 8pp.

The tramways of Accrington, 1886-1932, with brief notes on the adjoining systems of Blackburn, Darwen, Haslingden and Rawtenstall. RUSH, R.W. Light Railway Transport League, 1961, 88pp.

The first in the kingdom: a history of buses and trams in Blackburn and Darwen. FERGUSSON, R.P & OTHERS. Darwen Transport Group, 1981, 56pp.

British & Irish tramway systems since 1945. WALLER, M.H. & P. Ian Allan, 1992, 192pp. (Darwen, pp.55-56).

HASLINGDEN CORPORATION TRAMWAYS
Haslingden Corporation Tramways. *Tramway & Railway World,* vol.25, 4 February 1909, pp.99-101.

Haslingden Corporation Tramways. *Light Railway & Tramway Journal,* vol.20, 5 February 1909, pp.77-80.

The tramways of Accrington, 1886-1932, with brief notes on the adjoining systems of Blackburn, Darwen, Haslingden, and Rawtenstall. RUSH, R.W. Light Railway Transport League, 1961, 88pp.

LANCASTER TRAMWAYS
Lancaster Corporation Tramways. *Light Railway & Tramway Journal,* vol.8, 6 February 1903, pp.103-107.

Lancaster electric tramways. *Tramway & Railway World,* vol.13, 12 February 1903, pp.127-132.

Notes on an unusual network. PHILLIPS, D.F. *Modern Tramway,* vol.6, no.63, March 1943, p.27 (The Lancaster and Morecambe systems).

The Lancaster and Morecambe tramways. SHUTTLEWORTH, S. Oakwood Press, 1976, 42pp.

LYTHAM ST. ANNE'S CORPORATION TRAMWAYS
See the "Blackpool" section above.

MORECAMBE TRAMWAYS
Morecambe-Heysham: the first petrol cars in England. *Light Railway & Tramway Journal,* vol.26, 19 January 1912, pp.43-45.
Petrol-driven tramway car. *Engineer,* vol.111, 19 January 1912, p.78.
Petrol tramway cars at Morecambe. *Tramway & Railway World,* vol.31, 8 February 1912, pp.87-92.
Notes on an unusual network. PHILLIPS, D.F. *Modern Tramway,* vol.6, no.63, March 1943, p.27.
Petrol trams in Heysham. HARMER, R.M. *Buses Illustrated,* vol.7, no.30, March-April 1957, pp.69/72.
The Lancaster and Morecambe tramways. SHUTTLEWORTH, S. Oakwood Press, 1976, 42pp.

NELSON CORPORATION TRAMWAYS
Nelson electricity works and tramways. *Light Railway & Tramway Journal,* vol.6, 4 April 1902, pp.152-155.
British tramways recalled: Burnley-Nelson-Colne-Preston. *Trams,* no.23, October 1966, pp.15-19.

PRESTON CORPORATION TRAMWAYS
The electric tramways of Preston. *Tramway & Railway World,* vol.16, 8 December 1904, pp.540-545.
Preston Corporation Tramways. *Light Railways & Tramway Journal,* vol.12, 3 February 1905, pp.125-126.
Memories of Preston Corporation Tramways. GARTH, W.S. *Tramway Review,* vol.4, no.31, 1961, pp.205-207.
British tramways recalled: Burnley-Nelson-Colne-Preston. *Trams,* no.23, October 1966, pp.15-19.
The tramways of Preston. HEYWOOD, G.W. *Tramway Review,* vol.9, no.67, Autumn 1971, pp.67-77/92; vol.9, no.68, Winter 1971, pp.99-124; vol.9, no.69, Spring 1972, pp.131-146; vol.9, no.70, Summer 1972, pp.163-

167/181-191; vol.9, no.71, Autumn 1972, pp.207-212; vol.10, no.77, Spring 1974, pp.154-160.

Classic tramcars. WISEMAN, R.J.S. Ian Allan, 1986, 128pp, (Preston, pp.41-44).

Preston's trams and buses. RHODES, M. Venture Publications, 1995, 80pp.

RAWTENSTALL CORPORATION TRAMWAYS

Rawtenstall Corporation Tramways. *Tramway & Railway World*, vol.25, 6 May 1909, pp.341-347.

Rawtenstall Corporation Tramways: the last English steam tramway electrified. *Light Railway & Tramway Journal*, vol.20, 7 May 1909, pp.263-267.

Golden jubilee of Rawtenstall Corporation Transport Department, 1908-1958. RAWTENSTALL BOROUGH COUNCIL. 1958, 16pp.

The tramways of Accrington, 1886-1932, with brief notes on the adjoining systems of Blackburn, Darwen, Haslingden, and Rawtenstall. RUSH, R.W. Light Railway Transport League, 1961, 88pp.

C. OTHER TRAMWAYS

Blackpool North Pier Tramway. ORCHARD, A. Lancastrian Tramway Publications, 1993, 16pp.

Pier Railways & Tramways of the British Isles. TURNER, K. Oakwood Press, 1999, 80pp (Blackpool North Pier pp.6-7).

D. LIGHT RAIL SCHEMES

Little has been written about the proposed modernisation of the Blackpool tramway system, as the outcome of a bid for funding of a light rail scheme is still awaited. Some useful background material can be found in *"Tramways & Urban Transit"*, vol.64, no.765, September 2001, pp.324-325.

E. TRAMWAY MUSEUMS & PRESERVATION

Due to the fact that the majority of tramways in this area closed before the preservation movement became established, there are few surviving trams for enthusiasts and historians to view. Rawtenstall car 23 and a Carlisle tram are awaiting restoration at private locations, whilst the lower saloon of

Lytham St. Anne's car 43 has been adapted for use on the West Lancashire Light Railway at Hesketh Bank, near Preston.

However, the continued survival of the Blackpool tramway system has ensured that a large number of cars survives in preservation at home and abroad. The Crich Tramway Village (National Tramway Museum), Crich, near Matlock, Derbyshire, DE4 5DP, houses the largest collection, including the original open top conduit car of 1884, double deck bogie cars 40 and 49 of 1926, bogie toastrack car 166 of 1927, single deck car 167 of 1928, plus the 1927 steeple cab locomotive which was used to haul coal trains to Copse Road depot in Fleetwood. Blackpool & Fleetwood Tramroad crossbench bogie single deck car 2 of 1898 is also on view. Not currently on display are open top "Dreadnought" car 59 of 1902, and the much newer one-man operated car 5 of 1972.

The East Anglia Transport Museum, Chapel Road, Carlton Colville, near Lowestoft, Suffolk, NR33 8BL, has amongst its collection Blackpool "Standard" car 159 of 1929, plus English Electric 'Vambac' car 11 of 1939 which is currently being restored.

Restored Blackpool open top car 31 of 1901 is in working condition at The North of England Open Air Museum, Beamish, County Durham, DH9 0RG.

In addition, former one-man operated car 10 of 1975 is now used at the Wokefield Park Executive Training and Conference Centre near Reading as part of its catering and hospitality section, and is painted in Reading bus livery. Public access is not allowed at this location.

The Blackpool tramway system itself includes a number of restored trams, including "Standard" car 147 of 1924, which was repatriated to the UK from America in 2000, as well as former Blackpool & Fleetwood Tramroad Company single deck car 40 of 1914. Two of the 1952/1953 batch of "Coronation" cars are still to be found in working order, including car 304 which was the subject of a restoration project for the Channel 4 TV programme "Salvage Squad" in 2002. In addition many of the trams in everyday service are museum pieces in their own right, especially the famous "Balloon" cars and Brush "Railcoaches" from the 1930's, though a number have been substantially rebuilt in recent years.

The latest development in tramway preservation in the North-West surrounds the Lancastrian Transport Trust's plans to establish a transport museum in Blackpool, and it has already acquired a number of Blackpool trams including one-man operated car 8 of 1974, "Standard" car 143 of 1924, "Coronation" car 663 of 1953, as well as the illuminated "Rocket" car 732.

A number of Blackpool trams are also preserved in the United States. The Oregon Electric Railway Museum at Brooks, Oregon, operates the Willamette Shore Trolley Line and includes in its collection "Standard" car 48 of 1928. The former illuminated "Blackpool Belle" is also thought to be still at this location. "Standard" car 144 of 1925 resides at the Seashore Trolley Museum at Kennebunkport, Maine. Three of Blackpool's famous open "Boat" single deckers are also in the USA. Car 226 runs at the California Railway Museum at Rio Vista Junction; car 228 operates on the San Francisco tramway system, whilst the latest car to leave Blackpool for America is car 606 which moved to Trolleyville USA, Columbia Park, near Cleveland, Ohio in 2000 in exchange for the return of "Standard" car 147.

F. TRAMWAY MANUFACTURERS

The manufacture of rolling stock. *Tramway & Railway World*, vol.1, June 1892, pp.205-215 (Lancaster Railway Carriage & Wagon Company).
The Electric Railway and Tramway Carriage Works. *Railway World*, vol.8, 13 April 1899, pp.134-139 (Description of the Preston works).
'Little Olympia' at Preston: interesting exhibit of vehicles at Dick, Kerr Works. *Electric Railway, Bus & Tram Journal*, vol.71, 14 December 1934, pp.580-583.
The Dick, Kerr album. HYDE, W.G.S & PEARSON, F.K. 1972, 52pp. (Brief history of the English Electric Company's works at Preston).
Trams in the North-West. HESKETH, P. Ian Allan, 1995, 128pp (Ch.5 includes material on tram builders of Preston).
The Dick, Kerr story. PRICE, J.H. Tramway & Light Railway Society 1996, 64pp.
English Electric tramcar album. LUMB, G. Ian Allan, 1999, 128pp.

G. REFERENCE MATERIAL

1. BOOKS

A useful guide is Keith Turner's "Directory of British Tramways", published by Patrick Stephens in 1996, which contains potted histories of all British tramways.

Two annual publications from the Victorian era contained much useful statistical information, maps and accounts. These are "Duncan's Manual of Tramway Companies in the United Kingdom", published from 1877 to 1905, and "Garcke's Manual of Electrical Undertakings" published from 1898.

Town directories such as those published by Kelly's often contain tramway information, such as lists of operators and routes, though their frequency of publication varied, and in the years after the Second World War, they became less comprehensive.

2. PERIODICALS

The major British tramway periodicals are:

Railway World	1892-1899 continued as
Tramway & Railway World	1899-1934 continued as
Transport World	1934-1968
Light Railway & Tramway Journal	1899-1914 continued as
Electric Railway & Tramway Journal	1914-1927 continued as
Electric Railway Bus & Tram Journal	1927-1936 continued as
Passenger Transport Journal	1937-1946 continued as
Passenger Transport	1947-1968
Modern Tramway	1938-1991 continued as
Light Rail & Modern Tramway	1992-1997 continued as
Tramways & Urban Transit	1998 to date
Tramway Society Bulletin	1938-winter 1940 contd as
Tramway Bulletin	April 1940, then
Local Transport Magazine	June 1940, then
Tramway & Light Railway Members'	

Forum	April 1941-April 1942,
then	
Tramway Society Forum	6/1942 to 3-5/1944, then
Tramway Society Bulletin	Jan/Feb 1958-11/1965,
then	
The Bulletin	Winter 1966-5/85, then
The Bulletin & Tram Fare	1985 to date
Tramway Review	1950 to date
Trams	1961-1969

The major articles from all these periodicals are included in this bibliography, but many issues contain short paragraphs and news items which may be of interest to the enthusiast/historian.

In view of the popularity of the Blackpool tramway, it is not surprising that a number of periodicals have been produced which focus on developments on this particular system, including:

BLACKPOOL TRAMWAY PHOTO NEWS (edited by Nick Meskell)
No.1   Covering the period 2.1.1988-31.3.1988
No.2   Covering the period 1.4.1988-6.11.1988
No.3   Covering the period 7.11.1988-5.11.1989
Continued as
BLACKPOOL TRAMWAY YEARBOOK (edited by Nick Meskell)
No.4   Covering the period 6.11.1989-31.12.1990
No.5   Covering events in 1991

TRAMS PICTORIAL (edited by Nick Meskell)
No.1   2002

TRAMS (edited by Nick Meskell)
No.1   June 1998 to date   Quarterly

TRAMTRAX (edited by Nick Meskell)
No.1   January 1988 to ?   Monthly

FYLDE TRAMWAY NEWS (I)
October 1971-1980   Quarterly

FYLDE TRAMWAY SOCIETY NEWSLETTER
September 1976-1980   Monthly

FYLDE TRAMWAY NEWS (II)
No.1   September 1980 – date   Monthly

THE BLACKPOOL RAILCOACH
No.1   1970-date   Irregular
A news-sheet produced by Keith Terry on the restoration of Blackpool 298

3. NEWSPAPERS

Local newspapers are an invaluable source of information on such tramway matters as opening and closing ceremonies, accidents, senior staff appointments, resignations and deaths of tramway personnel etc. Unfortunately, very few newspapers are indexed, so the best approach is by consulting the files for a specific date. Local newspaper offices and libraries usually keep a file of the local paper, often going back decades. In most cases it is not possible to take photocopies from the original bound volumes, but the advent of microfilming has meant that many can now be copied on special machines thus saving hours of laborious note-taking.

4. LEGISLATION

Generally, tramways could be promoted in one of 3 ways, under:
Provisional Order of the Secretary of State, confirmed by Act of Parliament (Tramways Act 1870, ss.4 & 14)
Special private Act of Parliament incorporating Parts II and III of the Tramways Act 1870
Orders made by Commissioners under the Light Railways Act 1896, ("LRO") subject to confirmation by the Board of Trade but with no necessity for a confirming Act.
Where "etc." is used below, it signifies that other associated place names will be mentioned:
Accrington etc.

    45-6V.c.cxviii;   50-1V.c.lvi;   5E7.c.xliii.Pt.II;   6E7.c.xlix;
    18G5.c.xcv.Pt.III

Barrow-in-Furness etc.
44-5V.c.cxxi; 47-8V.c.cvii; 51-2V.c.lxiv; 57-8V.c.cxci;
3E7.c.cxlvi; 4E7.c.ci.Pt.IV; 15-6G5.c.cvii.Pt.III

Blackburn, etc
LRO 2.10.1901

Blackpool etc
LRO 14.6.1901; 14.1.1905; 47-8V.c.cxii; 43-4V.c.clxxiii; 56-7V.c.lxxxvi, cxciii, & ccxvi*; Pt.VIII; 59-60V.c.cxx, cxxix,* cxxx.s.9, & cxlvii; 60-1V.c.cli; 62-3V.c.clxxxiv, & cclxxix; 61-2V.c.cvi, & ccix*; 63-4V.c.ccxi*; 1E7.c.cxxviii.Pt.II; 5E7.c.clxxiii.Pt.III; 7-8G5.c.lii.Pt.III; 9-10G5.c.li.Pt.III; 10-11G5.c.liv.Pt.II, & lxxxiii; 13-4G5.c.lxxxvi; 15-6G5.c.cii; 25-6G5.c.cviii.Pt.IV; * = rep. by 13-4G5.c.lxxxvi.Sch.5

Burnley etc.
42-3V.c.cxciii; 45-6V.c.cxxxviii; 50-1V.c.cxcvi; 61-2V.c.cxcii; 63-4V.c.cxlix; 8E7.c.lxxxix; 11-2G5.c.xcii.Pt.V; 15-6G5.c.xcii.Pt.VII

Carlisle
43-4V.c.clxxiii; 61-2V.c.ccx

Colne etc
LRO 17.6.1901; 25.7.1902; 6.5.1903; 11-2G5.c.xlviii; 11-2G5.c.xlviii; 23-4G5.c.xxxv.Pt.VI

Darwen
62-3V.c.ccxxiv; 16-7G5.c.xi.Pt.II

Haslingden
6E7.c.xlix.Pt.II; 14-5G5.c.xlvii.Pt.III

Lancaster
52-3V.c.cx; 63-4V.c.ccxxxvi.Pt.II

Morecambe
49-50V.c.xxv; 55-6V.c.cxciv; 60-1V.c.clii; 9E7.c.cxliii; 10E7. & 1G5.c.xiii; 12-3G5.c.lii

Nelson – see Burnley

Preston etc.
39-40V.c.ccxiv; 41-2V.c.lii; 43-4V.c.clxii; 48-9V.c.xxxv; 61-2V.c.ccxii; 63-4V.c.cxlv.Pts.3 & 5; 2E7.c.lix.Pt.II; 3E7.c.ccxxxv; 4E7.c.lvi; 6E7.c.xxxiv; 9E7.c.xxxiv; 2-3G5.c.lxxvii; 4-5G5.c.lxii.Pt.IV; 21-2G5.c.xiii.Pt.IV

Rawtenstall
7E7.c.lxxvii; 10E7.&1G5.c.ci; 14-5G5.c.x.Pt.II

West Cumberland
1E7.c.ccli; 3E7.c.cviii; 5E7.c.viii

5. ACCIDENT REPORTS

Tramway operators, like railway operators, were under a duty to report accidents to the Board of Trade, later the Ministry of Transport, which, depending upon the seriousness, might order an enquiry. Prescribed forms were laid down by the Board of Trade. On 21st March 1904 a letter was issued from the Board setting out the types of electrical and general accident which had to be reported, e.g. Overhead work broken by trolley, or failure of insulation, "to be reported only if causing injury to any person, or if accompanied by heavy short circuit, or alarming result", while "all cases of cars running away should be notified, whether such accidents result in personal injury or not...."

The following accident reports were reprinted in the Journal of The Tramways and Light Railways Association:
Rawtenstall Corporation Tramways, report dated 22.11.1911 into accident on 11.11.1911 in Manchester Road, Accrington (car 14 got out of control on loop and collided with car 11, 20 passengers injured), pp.309-311.
Burnley Corporation Tramways, report dated 2.1.1920 into accident on 28.11.1919 (car 10 overturned on Briercliffe New Road hill, 4 passengers and one boy standing on pavement injured), pp.2111-2116).

6. TIMETABLES AND GUIDES

Most tramway systems produced timetables, and although some can still be found on stalls at transport rallies etc., those of the 1950's and before usually command high prices. Local libraries often keep back copies of old timetables, and examples can also be found on display in local museums.

7. MAPS

Maps of varying scales can provide useful information for tramway historians. Useful works are those published by G.L.Crowther:
"National series of waterways, tramway and railway atlases"

Vol. 2A	Central and North Lancashire	2001	80 pages	
Vol. 2B	Isle of Man/Furness/Westmoreland	1998	61 pages	47 maps
Vol. 2K	East Lancashire	2001	70 pages	
Vol. 2L	Cumberland	2001	61 pages	47 maps

Vol. 2S North-East Lancashire   2001   46 pages
Vol. 2U Lytham, Fleetwood & Blackpool   2001   75 pages

The 25" to 1 mile (1.2500) Ordnance Survey maps are also worthy of study. Although published at infrequent intervals, they are large enough in scale to show track layouts etc. Once again, libraries are usually able to provide relevant sheets for their areas.

8. COUNCIL MINUTES
The minutes of local authority tramway committees are usually extremely detailed, and can throw much light on the events and discussions leading up to fare increases, line closures, purchase of new rolling stock etc. In some cases they can provide information on track re-laying, and appointments of senior personnel. Council minutes are usually available at major reference libraries.

9. ANNUAL REPORTS
The annual reports of both public and privately-owned tramways are well worth searching out. Those for local authority tramways can be found in the local reference library, whilst those of company-owned lines may be located at the National Tramway Museum. They can be relied upon to give an accurate picture of the system during a particular year, often supported by a wealth of financial and statistical information.

10. TRADE LITERATURE
The catalogues of the major tramway builders, e.g. Hurst Nelson, Dick Kerr, Mountain and Gibson, are likely to be found at the National Tramway Museum. The advertisement pages of the various tramway trade journals can also be useful.

11. ARBITRATION/LITIGATION/LAW REPORTS
There is a wealth of information about tramways to be found in law reports and textbooks often held in solicitors' offices. Halsbury's Laws of England, which runs into many volumes, has a long section on tramways and light railways, e.g. volume 32 of the second edition devotes over 70 pages to the subject, and is a useful initial guide to relevant cases. For example: p.717, references to *Burnley Corporation v Lancaster County*

Council 1889, 54 J.P.279; 26 Digest 395, *1215*; also *Over Darwen Corporation v Lancaster County Justices* 1887, 58 L.T. 51; 26 Digest 396, (Re Tramways Act 1870 s.29 – scavenging). Also *Blackpool and Fleetwood Tramroad Co. v. Bailey*, 1920, 1K.B. 380; 43 Digest 347, *61* – re definition of hackney carriage within Town Police Clauses Acts. In volume 7 of the *Journal of the Municipal Tramways and Transport Association* of 1928, there are two interesting reports on actions for damages for personal injuries against Barrow-in-Furness Corporation Tramways; in the first, pp.537-538, damages of £1083 and £46 were awarded at Liverpool Assizes, but in the second, pp.615-616, the verdict and judgment were reversed by the Court of Appeal.

Other references to arbitration and litigation may be found in periodicals and newspapers, although these will often be summaries and condensed reports.

G. LIBRARY ADDRESSES

The John Price Memorial Library at the Crich Tramway Village (National Tramway Museum), Crich, Nr. Matlock, Derbyshire, DE4 5DP (Telephone 01773 852565) houses a vast collection of material relating to the tramways of Britain and abroad. None of this material is available for borrowing, but can be consulted by prior arrangement with the Librarian, Mrs. Rosemary Thacker.

The following libraries may have material relevant to the tramways in their areas:

ACCRINGTON
Accrington Library, St. James' Street, Accrington, BB5 1NQ

BARROW
Central Library, Ramsden Square, Barrow-in-Furness, Cumbria, LA14 1LL

BLACKBURN
Central Library, Town Hall Street, Blackburn, BB2 1AG

BLACKPOOL
Central Library, Queen Street, Blackpool, FY1 1PX

BURNLEY
Burnley Library, Grimshaw Street, Burnley, BB11 2BD

COLNE
Colne Library, Market Square, Colne, Lancashire, BB8 OAP

FLEETWOOD
Fleetwood Library, North Albert Street, Fleetwood, Lancashire, FY7 6AJ

LANCASTER
Lancaster Library, Market Square, Lancaster, LA1 1HY

LYTHAM
Lytham Library, 27 Clifton Street, Lytham St. Anne's, Lancashire, FY8 5EP

MORECAMBE
Morecambe Library, Central Drive, Morecambe, Lancashire, LA4 5DL

NELSON
Nelson Library, Market Square, Nelson, Lancashire, BB9 7PU

PRESTON
The Harris Library, Market Square, Preston, PR1 2PP

RAWTENSTALL
Rawtenstall Library, Queens Square, Haslingden Road, Rawtenstall, Lancashire, BB4 6QU

SOURCE BOOKS – PUBLISHING PROGRAMME:

Already published:
1.   Scotland [£5]
2.   Wales [£4]
3.   North-East England [£4]
4.   Yorkshire [£5.50]
5.   East Anglia [£4]
6.   South-Central England [£4]